Early Evening Pieces

Books by Marianne Bluger

The Thumbless Man

On Nights Like This

Gathering Wild

Summer Grass

Tamarack & Clearcut

Gusts: Selected Tanka

Scissor, Paper, Woman

Early Evening Pieces

Early Evening Pieces

by

Marianne Bluger

BuschekBooks

National Library of Canada Cataloguing in Publication

Bluger, Marianne
      Early evening pieces / Marianne Bluger.

Poems.
ISBN 1-894543-14-9

      I. Title.

PS8553.L85E27 2003   C811'.54   C2003-901587-4
PR9199.3.B58E27 2003

Front Cover Image: *Ottawa Experimental Farm*, Michael Adam Kim
Author Photo by Jessica A. Emory

The book is set in Giovanni Book and AGaramond.

Printed in Canada by Hignell Book Printing, Winnipeg, Manitoba.

BuschekBooks gratefully acknowledges the support of the Canada Council for
the Arts and the Ontario Arts Council for its publishing program.

BuschekBooks
P.O. Box 74053, 5 Beechwood Avenue
Ottawa, Ontario K1M 2H9
Canada
Email: buschek.books@sympatico.ca

Conseil des Arts
du Canada

Canada Council
for the Arts

ONTARIO ARTS COUNCIL
CONSEIL DES ARTS DE L'ONTARIO

for Larry

&

for my Mother

Some of these haiku have appeared previously in Canada in *Arc, Tidepool, raw nervz, New Cicada, Daybreak, Blue Jay, Haiku Canada Newsletter* and *Broadsheets*; in the U.S. in *Modern Haiku, Parnassus Literary Journal, Dasoku, Frogpond, The Heron's Nest*; in Japan in *Soul of the Seasons,* Ikkoku Santo, Ed.; *Asahi Evening News, Azami, Mainichi Daily News,* and in various anthologies.

Thanks to Rod Willmot and John Buschek for their kind exactitude in editing the poems.

With gratitude to Philip Barron, Alexander Tran, Andrew Hrnchiar and Jonathan Yau.

I thank the Regional Municipality of Ottawa Carleton and Ontario Arts Council for grants to write poetry.

Contents

SWEETGRASS

in a pause
when the wind dies
the coo of a dove

the moonlit station
empty as a train whistles
through the small town

pearly dawn
the snail on a frond turns
its glistening horn

the woodland darkens
one by one whip-poor-wills
take up the sweet plaint

star-pierced darkness...
clear and close
a cricket chirps

deep in sweetgrass
my net again misses
the butterfly

storm blowing my boat
sidelong in rushes
bent white with wind

through drifting mist
croak of ravens
changing perches in a spruce

a bittern calls
sunburnt arms
lift binoculars

                              picnic speeches...
                              crumb by crumb
                              the ants

far shore
rattle of a kingfisher
fades into stillness

                              the wood duck preens
                              with delicate movements
                              I adjust the scope

a grouse settles
in the spindly spruce—
last call of a thrush

sunset lingers
by the mountain lake
we sip smoky tea

under blue heaven
on sweet clover heat haze
butterflies swim

lonesome backroad
sunset burning
the pines char black

the gorge at dawn
its ancient pines afloat
on tiers of mist

soft summer darkness
resting the oars I glide
on floating stars

a hairstreak
     clinging
          to a sedge in the wind

a bee in the kitchen...
drifting through screens
apple blossom sweetness

noon heat
shadow of a hawk
crosses the clearcut

warm blueberries
along a sand path winding
into sunset

as I write field notes
a glittering green beetle
inspects my ankle

(in my coffee mug
as I polished these poems
a midge drowned)

HIGHWAY WIND

blue sky—
ping of a tollbooth quarter
lights up GO

with enviable impudence
a swallowtail sails over
the customs turnstile

the remains
under roadside pines
of someone's McLunch

cheerful mechanic
sketches the broken fuel pump
on my map

passing through
a smalltown mainstreet
into darkness

all night
transport headlights
panning this 20 buck room

one by one
looming up through mist
hydro pole crosses

highway wind
whipping the fur
of a farm dog's corpse

a sunshower—
splashed by a passing transport
I steer blind

speeding...
faint *tic* as a monarch
hits the windshield

in sun on the Main
language cops measuring
an English sign

spray-painted black
on a gilt gothic church sign
"101"

in traffic tied
upright on a flat-bed truck
one Louis Quatorze chair

on a combine
rusting in prairie grass
the falcon rests

Stoney grasslands
a homestead—roofless
under low-slung cloud

one little breeze
and the sagebrush starts
whispering to the stars

August
at the look-out on horseback
a Blackfoot

                         cars flashing up
                         a mountain turnpike
                         into sunset

cold rain
lashing clearcut and that sulphur
stink of mills

                         caught
                         in a Klondike sandbar
                         the ribcage of a horse

lost and trying
to refold the map
I spot the peak

vine-choked ruins
beside the black waters
where dragonflies hover

leaves drifting
down at the corner
a bus disappears

all the way down
to an old quarry pond
rubbish in the rain

FLIGHT

wind in the trees
tonight by one bare bulb
I pack the shadows

flight delayed
the mist keeps rolling in
against the glass

by the pay phone
forgotten
an address book

at take-off
the guy on the aisle
deep in his thriller

the stewardess leans
well-groomed and loving
to be looked at

at the pilot's calm
voice on the intercom
an infant screams

the drink trolley tinkles
my seatmate returns
make-up perfect

by her diamond stud
the line
where her pancake ends

inflight movie
cloud fluff
we bump through...

in headphones
the passengers laughing together
all suddenly stop

middle of the night
miles above Earth
tackling customs forms

gleaming dimly
in cabin lamps—three hundred
human heads

the cabin lamp's
narrow beam focused
on a pocket romance

falling through night
with a lunge we tilt
toward a grid of light

lights turning on
faces stunned
the flight is done

3 a.m.
the conveyor turning
one battered green valise

GOLDENROD & ASTERS

the woodland grapes
have darkened—on the hillside
goldenrod gleams

        through sunshafts
           yellow leaves drift
               to a slow-flowing river

bumper to bumper
for the autumn colour—
I lose my temper

        that gash
        on granite of scarlet
        sumac

a leaf floats—
into the gorge where a boxcar rusts
mountain silence

                                        from an aspen
                                        the north wind shakes
                                        a finch flies

under bare trees
the painter's cabin
nearly lost in leaves

                                        sunless cold
                                        stubble-field jig of a scarecrow
                                        twisting in wind

early dark
against the chill
a front door closes

cancer weakness
through glass I watch gusts
shift the dry leaves

under naked trees
a junco goes
rustling the silence

dusk
a gleam on the last
copper chrysanthemum

brown leaves
skirling in the drained canal
a broken bicycle

black ribbon
of a squirrel's tail waving
through October trees

bong bong of a bell
and the rain
falling on stone

past ghostly factories
moonlit   shimmering
the black river flows

hands stiff with cold
raking leaves in the wind
I miss my kids

rustling dry leaves
a squirrel busy
where I planted crocus

on a gnarled branch
in the bitter cold—wild apples
gold with sunset

bagpipes wheeze
through the cenotaph mist
a thin line of vets

frozen in mud
a footprint—out of nowhere
the first flakes fly

opening slowly
in the warm kitchen   the last
frost-scarred red rose

SNOWBLIND

first frost
by the tire store—a chipwagon's
hot grease smell

swings stir
in an empty playground
snowflakes fly

hail pounds the roof
up into rafter shadows
he slides my old canoe

crow in his elm
& me in the attic
watching snowflakes whirl

the basket chair
its cushion
snow

kicking snowblind
through drifts to the shed
where a shovel waits

stuck in a snowbank
with nothing in the trunk
but my butterfly net

across windswept ice
that white shape through my scope
a snowy owl

sun blue—
tap of an empty milkweed pod
on dazzling snowcrust

Saturday night
bath running & the hockey game
in overtime

eyes bright
with pneumonia Grandma quips
"What next?"

sudden ruckus—
sparrows in a cedar
knocking snow off

this luminous quiet
night sharp stars
and woodsmoke

> the carillon ringing
> snowflakes
> into the Eternal Flame

out the window
on a ladder—the cableman
blurred by blizzard

> the plow churns past
> beyond a snowbank
> bobs the postman's cap

the last ember dies
a chill takes the house
by moonlight

                              night falling
                              and nothing written
                              but five bitter lines

sunny sub-zero
my shovel scrapes
starlings waver in chimney heat

                              on black ice
                              the ridiculous dance
                              before my ass lands

dawn flash
off a lone skater's blades
hissing down the canal

                              lifted to touch
                              the Christmas star—baby niece
                              smiles through her tears

back home
to snowprints—someone's
come and gone

                              waking with a start
                              to quiet—
                              moonlight floods the room

the queen too
on our stamps
a little older

in my shabby room
on the dusty palm
sun

the long dash
one o'clock—still in her corner
that winter spider

GUSTS

coatless in mist
I shovel the last heavy
honey-combed snow

trickle of spring
meltwater over
a dime in the gutter

bright moonlight
tail straight up the neighbour's cat
sniffs our trash

on bare sidewalk
my shoe grinding winter
grit underfoot

fine rain
soaking in the puddle
a red wool mitt

in spring wind—
touching my nipples
cold silk

rippling the sky
in flooded fields—swirling
larks ascend

visible again
leaf-lost trails
in soft spring rain

tulip buds tight
a robin in the rain
stretches a worm

spring twilight
above the traffic
geese honk

snow-melt trickles
where the fiddleheads are
poking old leaves up

a clap of thunder—
catching hands
we race the amber

thick fog tonight
the neighbour's dog
barks in confusion

                                            considering
                                            all the reasons to work
                                            I go out for a walk

singing somewhere
in this unravelling mist
a thrush

                                            spring peeper chorus
                                            swallowed by a deep-throat
                                            bullfrog gulp

wheelless in weeds
down the bootlegger's path
a rusty schoolbus

warm rain
at the lagoon duckweed bright
and redwings calling

Ash Wednesday
as I dust the piano
faint notes

icy rain...
staunch and frail
the daffodils brighten

sun lights the mist
by the river a redstart
flits through a willow

                            hazy pink
                            cloud at the burnt farm
                            a cherry in bloom

through soft night rain
a hound leads his big man swinging
a little plastic bag

                (avec un clin d'oeil à Dorothy Howard)

                            in the gnarled peach
                            some chirping thing
                            shakes the blossoms

through the willow-veiled
arch of an old stone bridge
ducklings

            spring cleaning...
            my lost watch
            in a summer skirt

on the porch screen
mayflies dying—their wings
fold and unfold

            chilly dawn
            song of a water thrush
            burnishes bare woods

over the small-town
bleachers filling for a game
a new spring moon

in the field
where I found that rare moth
they are moving the earth

on the market sidewalk
its roots in burlap—a sapling
crab in bloom

the sun sets—
flashing through lowertown
a commuter express

restless
this first warm night of bawling cats
and lilacs

swallows
flutter off the puddle
clouds appear

the moving van leaves
apple petals swirling
over the drive

that garbage truck
roaring off into drizzle
leaves my broken ladder

with every gust
the torn kite leaps
on the power line

the TV screen
in morning sun
dust-sheened

in the rain
at the curb—fashion mags
tied with panty hose

ANNAPOLIS

our engine fading
by the mountain & the valley
farm unchanged

                  as the farmer slops pigs
                  clouds drag their dapple
                  shade across the hills

warm wind
stroking the lowland grasses
blows my long hair free

                  lightning forks
                  through dark clouds a swallow
                  rides the wind

speck of a kite...
over endless grasslands
the wind in waves

Ma in her specs
spreads the *Globe* and starts
peeling carrots

the phone stops ringing...
slowly above the woodstove
the flypaper turns

all down the back road
escaped from Sprigg's farm
lupins bloom

drone of a jet
receding
in the haysweet afternoon

those pegs on the line
slanting west at twilight?
swallows

the barn cats doze—
above the neighbour haying
a kestrel rocks

the hens cluck past
old Beau on the backporch
shifts in doggy dream

golden dusk—
slowed up behind a haycart
we count bobolinks

a breeze
in the timothy—a swallowtail
flutters

apples turning red...
the smell of fresh-cut
wood in every yard

weaving
past hayfields a farm kid
bikes into sunset

silhouettes
in the sunset cows on a hill
file home to their barn

in rose-dimmed dusk
Pa still scything
under the apple trees

the barn lights go off
under stars   Pa
swings the big door closed

through the rain
Ma still waving in rearview—
we pull away

SUMMER QUILT FOR A WINTER NIGHT
(Helen's Poem)

traditional construction
natural dyes and fibres
16 blocks in four panels

in the cosmos
dancing
Cabbage Whites

summer evening
as I iron—faintly scorched
the scent of him

weaving
through buttercups
a split-rail fence

poplars shimmer
on warm sand a vixen
suckles young

o pibbity pibbity pibbity
goes a sparrow's heart-rending
hymn to blazing August

rain-rinsed twilight
a motionless toad
claims the path

tail cocked
swaying on a stem—a wren
sings up the sun

the heat...
among roses
a straw hat dips

over golden fields
of afternoon—milkweed down
drifting

with a gentle look
six-foot son
strokes his little cat

through the pines
soft breezes shifting
the stars

drum of rain
in the cabin
glow of kerosene

end of the dirt track
by a tar-paper shack
blue gentians

among the rushes
moonlight silvering
a path for my canoe

utterly still
the ragged heron
in a sparkling shoal

on the evening breeze
scent of my neighbour's
trembling sweet-peas

DUNEGRASS

foggy dawn
feel of cold wet sand
on my naked sole

village mainstreet
one end, the sea—the other
burning sky

twinkling
ocean eyes & horizon grins
of Digby fishermen

a horse canters
down the beach—soundless
in the roar of surf

past a reactor
gilded with sunset—a gull
wings back to the sea

every few seconds
offshore through warm night mist
a faint flash

in ruddy pools
the shorebirds'
long wavering legs

out watching terns
veer under windblown cloud
anchored by nothing...

above the swimmers
sandpipers cry
in August departing...

a cloud crosses the sun
the girl in the bikini
frowns

by the mariner's church
daybreak glinting
off an empty fifth

first light
hits the cliff—the gannets
lift

old clapboard hotel
shuttered for winter
forever

        the sun sparkles
        an eider bobs
        by sea-smashed rocks

immaculate
on a rusting barge
seagulls preen

        ceaseless winds
        at the lighthouse & gravestones
        with no names

from the empty beach
a crow flaps shouting through
le beau Buctouche

never before to sea
the young woman
embroiders furiously

outport kid
watching tourists reboard
kicks a rock

sea squall
on the empty deck
a pop can rolls

along the dunes
only wind in sea grass
& a ruined villa

tide's out
and the village heart's
a mudflat

on the beach
back to the wind—I watch it
sweep my tracks